Aunt Marcia,

Thank you for your constant love and support of Gaston and his mission! I love you always!

AuthorHouse™
1663 Liberty Drive
Bloomington, IN 47403
www.authorhouse.com
Phone: 1 (800) 839-8640

© 2015 Shannon Rae. All rights reserved.

No part of this book may be reproduced, stored in a retrieval system,
or transmitted by any means without the written permission of the author.

Published by AuthorHouse 4/23/2015

ISBN: 978-1-5049-0727-9 (sc)
ISBN: 978-1-5049-0728-6 (e)

Print information available on the last page.

Any people depicted in stock imagery provided by Thinkstock are models,
and such images are being used for illustrative purposes only.
Certain stock imagery © Thinkstock.

This book is printed on acid-free paper.

Because of the dynamic nature of the Internet, any web addresses or links contained in this book may have changed since publication and may no longer be valid. The views expressed in this work are solely those of the author and do not necessarily reflect the views of the publisher, and the publisher hereby disclaims any responsibility for them.

authorHOUSE®

Eastie Frog

and the Super Secret

Once upon a lily pad far away, lived a family of frogs.

There was a daddy frog, a mommy frog, and four little baby frogs.

The Frog family was like any other family when they played and laughed together.

They liked to watch each other
do things that they enjoyed.

This is their story.

WELCOME TO OUR
POND
COME FOR THE WATER
STAY FOR THE FUN

Gogi Frog was the oldest of the Frog babies.

He could play any sport imaginable!

His favorite sport was **BASEBALL**.
He could hit that ball all the way out of the park!

Gogi could tell you anything you needed to know about baseball players, anyone from the Yankees "Colossus of Croak" to the Red Sox "Big Hoppy".

His family loved to cheer him on as they watched him slide into home... **SAFE!**

Addi Frog was the next Frog baby.

She was creative

and kind

and **ever so clever.**

Her favorite thing to do was write her own songs and act in plays at the Pond Community Theater.

Her family sat proudly and watched their little froglet **SHINE,** as she moved across the stage with such ease.

The next froglet in the Frog family is **Morgie Frog.** Morgie is always excited about life and spends most of her time skipping to her own tune!

She's also a
BEAUTIFUL
dancer!

The Frog family can't help but smile seeing Morgie in all her glory.

And that brings us to the baby of the Frog family.

Eastie Frog can't hit a baseball like his big brother, Gogi. And he can't write like Addi, or dance like Morgie.

But he loves his family very much and is so proud of his talented brother and sisters.

The Frog family knows how lucky they are to have such an **AMAZING** little froglet brother who loves with his whole heart...

even when he's hurting.

You see, **Eastie Frog** is sick,
 and he's been sick for a very long time.

His legs don't work
 like the other frogs in the pond.

He won't be able to hop on his own.

Eastie spends much of his time going to the doctor,
 taking lots of **icky** medicine, and even
staying overnight at the hospital.

One day, when the three other frog children
 were leaving school for the day,
they noticed that Grandma was coming
 to pick them up instead of
 Mommy Frog.

Now, the froglets loved their **Grandma Frog** very much, but they knew what it meant when Mommy wasn't there to pick them up.

Eastie was in the hospital again...

"**No!**" cried Addi Frog.

"**This isn't fair!**" complained Gogi Frog.

"**I WANT MY MOMMY BACK!**" exclaimed Morgie Frog.

The little froglets were angry
   and scared
      and sad,
but they also knew that they loved
   their little brother froglet *so much*
   and they knew he needed to be
      in the hospital with Mommy right now.

The next day, Gogi frog had a big baseball game.

His team was playing for the **CHAMPIONSHIP!**

As he walked up to take his turn at bat, he looked back into the stands.

Mommy Frog still wasn't there.

She had stayed with Eastie at the hospital.

Gogi cheered for his teammates
and did his **very best** that day.

The team won the
championship
and carried him off the field
after the his game-winning
HOME RUN.

Although he was very happy
for himself and his team, he wished
he could look in the stands and see
his family sitting together and celebrating with him.

Later that evening, Addi and Morgie Frog were in a special play together. Addi had the lead role and Morgie was one of the amazing dancers in the show.

They were **so excited** to be doing something they loved, but as they peeked through the curtains and looked out into the audience, they noticed the empty chairs.

Mommy was still with Eastie, and Daddy Frog was standing in the back so that he could leave quickly after the show..

...and get back to the hospital.

The frog children
missed being a family.

They missed being together
and cheering for one another.

So if Eastie couldn't
be on the baseball team,
or dance with friends,

THEY would be HIS TEAM!

They made cards and posters to decorate his hospital room.

They called him **SuperE** and drew pictures of their favorite little froglet wearing a *bright red cape.*

When they got to visit him in the hospital, they made sure to be on their best behavior and wore masks to keep from making Eastie sick.

After many, many days in the hospital,

little **Eastie Frog** was ready to come home.

The whole pond was so excited!

They dressed up in capes and made signs and even organized a parade to welcome home their **HERO!**

The little froglets were in the front row, cheering louder than ever before.

Gogi decided that this moment was bigger than a homerun. Addi and Morgie agreed that no standing ovation could ever compare to having their **FAMILY TOGETHER AGAIN!**

After the parade, **Mayor Duck** asked Eastie to say a few words.

"We'd like to welcome you back to the Pond, Eastie!

You're our **HERO!**"

He handed the microphone to Mommy Frog who cradled Eastie in her arms.

Eastie cleared his little froggy throat, and began to speak.

"Thank you so much for the kind welcome. I know you're all here to see a hero, and I would like to introduce them to you now."

All the pond animals were confused.

"Them?" asked Otter.

"There is only ONE SuperE." said Turtle.

"Why did he say 'THEM'?" wondered the fish.

Eastie Frog smiled and asked for his brothers and sisters to stand next to him on the stage. Then, he explained, "Sometimes we call someone a hero when we can see that they are sick and working very hard to get better.

But we cannot forget that being a hero doesn't mean fighting a sickness and whether or not you get better.

Being a hero only means one thing, **LOVE."**

(Although Eastie Frog was very sick,
he was also very wise and he knew the
most important secret.)

He continued, "You see, I spend a lot of time in the hospital.
And that doesn't just mean that I'm sick.
It also means my **FAMILY** doesn't get to
BE TOGETHER.
Mommy and Daddy Frog take very good care of me,
but they have to miss homeruns
and ballerina twirls
and leading roles.

My brother and sisters are sad and angry sometimes
because we don't get to be together.

But it's okay to feel that way,
because I am sad and angry too.

"I miss my family when we are not together.

But I **KNOW** that no matter **WHERE I AM**, they always **LOVE** me.

When they come to see me in the hospital, **THEY are my medicine.**

I save my **BEST smiles** for them.

They love me enough to give me the time I need with Mommy Frog, even though they miss her.

LOVE is the best medicine and it's what makes **REAL heroes!**

I hope that no matter what, my froglet siblings know how much **I LOVE THEM** and **I'M SO PROUD** to be their little froglet brother.

And someday I hope to become a **REAL hero** just like them, and teach the world to **LOVE.**"

CPSIA information can be obtained at www.ICGtesting.com
Printed in the USA
LVOW05s0353140515

438245LV00026BA/323/P